Activity Book for

Sefer Ha-Aggadah

The Book of Legends for Young Readers

Volume 1: Bible Legends

Written and Illustrated by
ANN D. KOFFSKY

UAHC Press • New York

Name _____

School _____

Class _____

1 • Light and Fire

Uh oh! A bunch of words are missing from the page of your "book." Fortunately, these words have been found and now appear at the bottom of this page as scraps of paper. Use the words in those scraps to fill in the blank spaces in your "book."

_____ was the name of the first man. _____ was the

name of the first woman. Their first home was the _____ of

_____. The _____ convinced them to make the world's

first mistake, and they ate from the _____. As a punishment, they

had to leave home. After leaving, they were very scared because it started to get

_____, but they felt better when they saw the _____ and

the _____. God called the seventh day _____ and made

it a day of _____.

Adam	tree	Garden	rest	stars	snake	Eve

dark	Shabbat	moon	Eden

1

FCUS QUESTIONS

People are often named for a reason. Adam was called "Adam" because *adam*, which in Hebrew means "earth," was made from the earth. Eve's Hebrew name is *Chava*, which means "life." She was called "life" because she was the mother of all living people. Now it's your turn to answer some questions about names.

Ask your parents how much time they spent thinking about a name for you. They probably thought about it for a long time. Why did they pick the name they chose for you?

Do you have a Hebrew name? What does it mean?

Were you named for a specific person? Why were you named after that person?

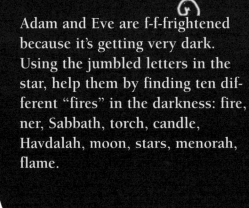

Adam and Eve are f-f-frightened because it's getting very dark. Using the jumbled letters in the star, help them by finding ten different "fires" in the darkness: fire, ner, Sabbath, torch, candle, Havdalah, moon, stars, menorah, flame.

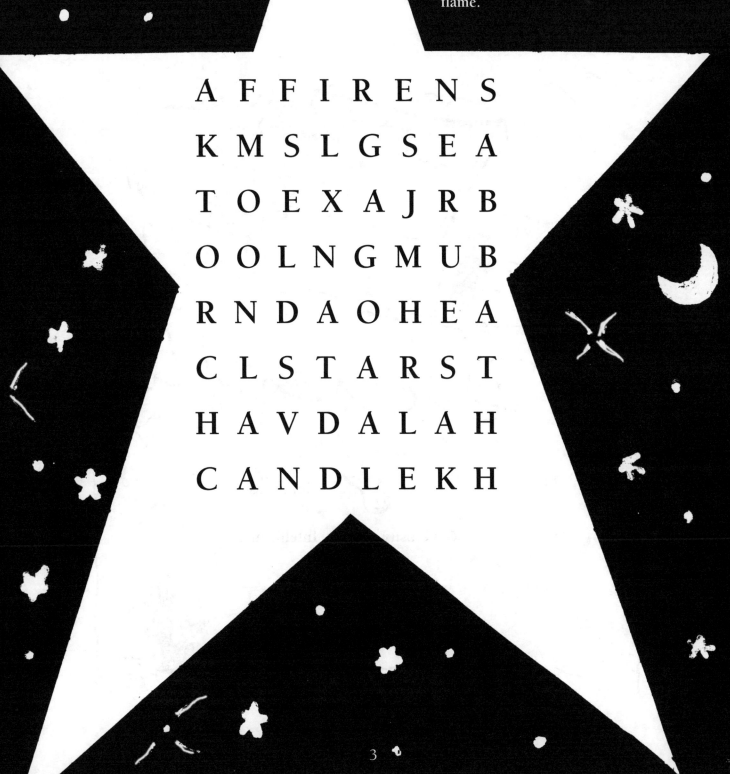

A F F I R E N S
K M S L G S E A
T O E X A J R B
O O L N G M U B
R N D A O H E A
C L S T A R S T
H A V D A L A H
C A N D L E K H

The Lie and Wickedness made a pair that was good enough to board Noah's ark. Now it's your turn to be matchmaker. Which qualities in the list below do you think would get along well together? Match up the qualities to form pairs by drawing a line between each pair. There are no right or wrong answers, but be prepared to explain your matches.

Love   Trust   Violence

Evil   Goodness

Generosity   Intelligence

Bravery

Fear   Cowardice

It's a hot news day at the *THE NEW OOPS TIMES*, and its staff is busy with all the mistakes made by the characters in this chapter of *Sefer Ha-Aggadah*. Help out the staff by writing the front page articles for them.

The New Oops Times

VOL. I   GENESIS   FREE

PEOPLE FROM BABEL ARE BABBLING

ADAM AND EVE MAKE THE WORLD'S FIRST MISTAKE

SNAKE PUNISHED

DRAW A "PHOTO" OF THE STORY "PEOPLE FROM BABEL ARE BABBLING."

"People Are Babbling" *continued*

"Adam and Eve..." *continued*

2 • How Shall You Be Blessed?

More missing words from your "book" have suddenly turned up in more scraps of paper. Fill in the blank spaces below with words from the scraps at the bottom of this page.

God wanted to bless Abraham and Sarah, but they already possessed three good

qualities: _____, _____, and _____.

Therefore, to help God decide how to bless them, an _____ told a

story about a _____ that grew in the wilderness. A wandering man

was grateful for its _____ and blessed it so that it would have good

offspring. Using this story as an example, God decided to bless Abraham and

Sarah with _____ who would be just like their _____.

tree   wisdom   angel   shade   children

honesty   love   parents

God has given each of us wonderful blessings. When we receive a blessing, just as when we get a present, it is nice to say thank you. Our rabbis wrote special thank yous for us to say whenever we received a blessing. They called these special thank yous (not coincidentally) "blessings." Match the "blessings" to the appropriate pictures.

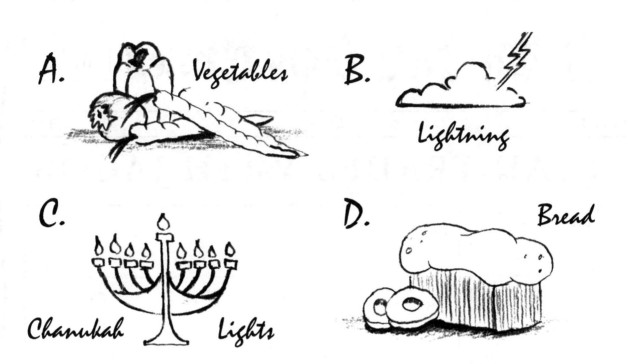

A. Vegetables

B. Lightning

C. Chanukah Lights

D. Bread

1. Blessed is *Adonai* our God, Ruler of the universe, Creator of the fruit of the earth._____

2. Blessed is *Adonai* our God, Ruler of the universe, who causes bread to come forth from the earth._____

3. Blessed is *Adonai* our God, Ruler of the universe, the Source of creative power._____

4. Blessed is *Adonai* our God, Ruler of the universe, who performed miracles for our ancestors in days of old, at this season._____

Another edition of THE NEW OOPS TIMES is hot off the presses. Once again the front page article isn't ready. Help out the staff by writing the article about Esau and Jacob before the paper hits the newsstand.

ALL MISTAKES ARE FIT TO PRINT

The New Oops Times

WEATHER: Good for Hunting

VOL. II   GENESIS   FREE

ESAU TRADES WITH JACOB

BY _____
(Your Name)

DRAW A "PHOTO" OF THE STORY "ESAU TRADES WITH JACOB"

Just as countries today have a flag, most countries in biblical times had similar banners. Generally, a flag indicates some feature that is meaningful for that country. Now that you know about Jacob and Esau, you know they can't share a flag. They're just too different! For each brother, design a flag that expresses his character and values.

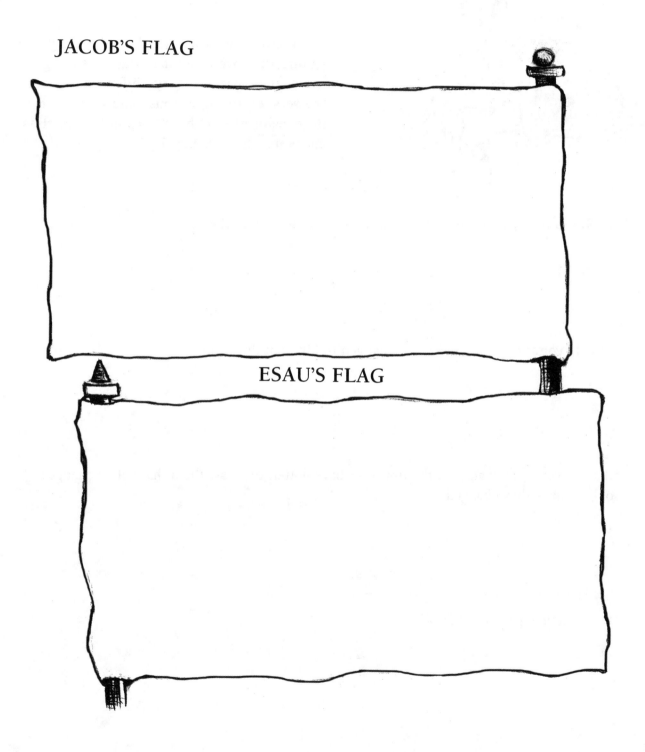

JACOB'S FLAG

ESAU'S FLAG

F CUS QUESTIONS

We know that when Jacob and Esau were young, they were similar. But as they grew older, they became very different. By your answers to the questions below, show how they changed and how you and your classmates may have changed.

Do you think Esau changed slowly or quickly? In what way did he change?

Why do you think Esau and Jacob changed in different directions?

Observe your classmates. In the time you have gotten to know them, have they changed? If so, how have they changed?

Have you changed at all? How?

3 • What Is a Promise Worth?

Missing words have again been found. Fill in the blank spaces in your "book."

Although Joseph had done nothing wrong, he was put in _____ in Egypt.

One day, he was released and asked to interpret the_____ of the Egyptian

ruler, who was called _____. Joseph was so successful that the

_____ and _____ in the court grew jealous. They insisted

Joseph be _____ to see if he knew the different languages spoken in Egypt.

After Joseph proved he could speak all the languages of Egypt, he tried to teach

Pharaoh the _____ language. After Pharaoh found that language too

difficult, he made Joseph promise not to tell anyone.

Pharaoh

tested

magicians

Hebrew

astrologers

prison

dreams

F⬡CUS QUESTIONS

Making a promise is a very big commitment. When we break a promise, it is difficult to get others to trust us again. Joseph realized this when Pharaoh asked Joseph to break his promise to his father. Now you have a chance to answer some questions about promises.

Do you ever make promises? What kind of promises have you made?

Did you keep those promises?

Did anyone ever promise you something and then not keep the promise? How did that make you feel?

How do you think Joseph felt when Pharaoh asked him to break his promise to Jacob?

Pharaoh is testing Joseph to see if he knows the unusual language that appears on this page. Help Joseph by translating what Pharaoh is saying.

Yikes! The new Pharaoh has tricked the Jews! But instead of bricks, Pharaoh wants you to make as many words as possible from the letters in the phrase *Let My People Go*. He wants them done in five minutes. Go!

LET MY PEOPLE GO

1. _____   11. _____

2. _____   12. _____

3. _____   13. _____

4. _____   14. _____

5. _____   15. _____

6. _____   16. _____

7. _____   17. _____

8. _____   18. _____

9. _____   19. _____

10. _____   20. _____

The seven women at the well were saved because an Egyptian forced Moses to flee Egypt. What made that Egyptian force Moses to flee? What led to that event? Starting with the picture of Moses at the well, connect the pictures in the maze below in reverse order to see the events that preceded your starting point.

4 • Loving the Small Things

Somebody is really careless with the words in your "book." Patch up this page to complete your story.

God was impressed with how much Moses cared about small things and decided to

speak to Moses from a tree. At first all the trees and bushes wanted God to speak from

them. The _____ tree thought God should speak to Moses from it because

it provided Moses with _____ from its roots when he wandered through

the _____. The _____ tree argued that it should speak to

Moses because part of it was used in the flour for the _____ at Moses' mar-

riage feast. But God chose the _____ to show that even something that

does not seem important is valuable in God's eyes.

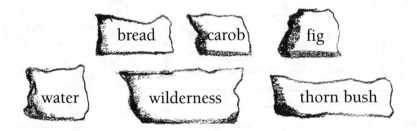

16

Most of the time, we think that bigger is better. But God picked a lowly thorn bush from which to speak to Moses when he had saved a tiny lamb. Keep a journal for a week of small things people do for you and small things you do for other people.

JOURNAL OF "SMALL THINGS"

Sunday _____

_____

Monday _____

_____

Tuesday _____

_____

Wednesday _____

_____

Thursday _____

_____

Friday _____

_____

Shabbat _____

_____

_____

FCUS QUESTIONS

God chose the thorn bush to speak to Moses in order to show that even the smallest things are important parts of God's world, especially those small kindnesses we show others. Consider the questions below, which relate to doing small things.

From your journal, choose two small things that people did for you. What difference did these things make to you?

From your journal, choose two small things that you did for others. Was it hard for you to do them?

Do you think doing them made a difference to the person for whom you did them?

How did you feel doing them?

WBIB, the Bible TV news station, has just sent journalist Scoop Aggadah to cover the breaking story of the burning bush. Unfortunately, Scoop always seems to have equipment failures, and we can't get a clear picture on our TV screen. Behind Scoop, draw the scene of the burning thorn bush so viewers can tune in to this fantastic sight.

Pretend for a moment that you are an executive at Pyramid Advertising, a prestigious Egyptian ad agency. God has just approached you to market matzah as the ultimate travel food. Design a poster that advertises matzah as a great product. Now get out there and sell, sell, sell!

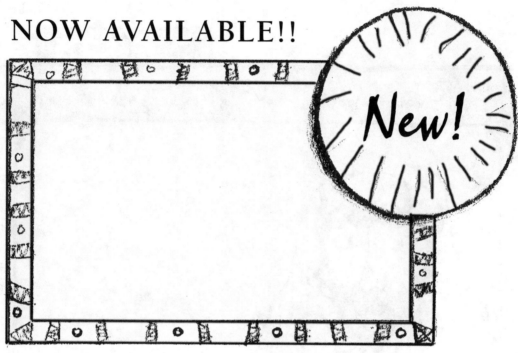

Draw a "photo" of the product to be sold.

List 3 selling points.

It _____!

It _____!

It _____!

 This Message Is Brought to You by Pyramid Advertising.

5 • A Time to Pray, A Time to Act

As you've done in earlier chapters, fill in the blank spaces with the words in the scraps below.

After the _____ plagues, Pharaoh decided to let the Children of Israel go free. But then he changed his mind. He and his soldiers got into their _____ to chase after the Israelites. They trapped the Israelites at the _____ of _____. When the Israelites grew frightened, Moses began to _____. But no one moved except for _____, who was from the tribe of _____. Because he had faith that God would help, he walked into the sea up to his _____. Finally, the sea split and the Children of Israel walked across on _____ land.

pray   Judah   Sea   chariots   ten

nose   Reeds   dry   Nahshon

21

FOCUS ON PRAYERS OF PRAISE

After the Jews crossed the Sea of Reeds safely, they praised God for saving them. Many of the prayers we say today also praise God, and many of the authors of these prayers used the letters in their name to start each line. In this way, their name could be read down the side of the prayer. This technique is called an acrostic. Write your own acrostic prayer, using your name to praise God. Below is an example that uses my name.

Amazing is God whose very

Name is wonderful.

Nothing can compare with the name of God.

_____

_____

_____

_____

_____

_____

_____

Because of one man's action, the Jews made it to the other side of the Sea of Reeds. Guide these letters through the sea to find out who that man was.

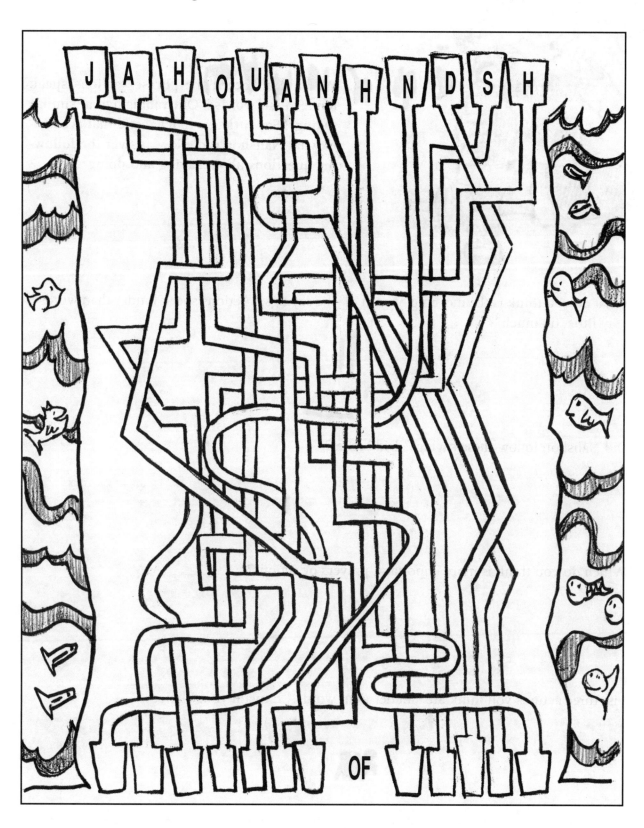

FCUS QUESTIONS

We have all heard the phrase "actions speak louder than words." Our rabbis had a similar saying: "Say little, do much," and that is exactly what Nahshon did. Now answer the following questions about saying and doing:

What do you think is the meaning of each of the sayings: "Actions speak louder than words"; "Say little, do much"?

Did Nahshon follow these sayings? Did Moses?

Which do you think is more important, prayers or actions?

List three actions you think are "louder than words." Explain your choices.

Pyramid Advertising has been hired by God once again. This time the ad agency is going to promote manna as the ultimate desert snack. Design a poster that will sell the Jews on the unique benefits of a balanced meal of manna.

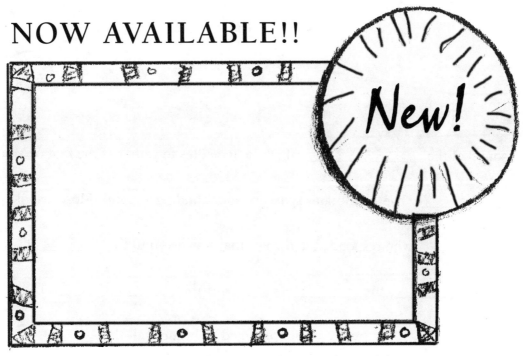

NOW AVAILABLE!!

New!

Draw a "photo" of the product to be sold.

List 3 selling points.

It _____!

It _____!

It _____!

 This Message Is Brought to You by Pyramid Advertising.

6 • God's Marvelous Voice

Again you're missing parts of your "book." And again, you will need to fill in the missing spaces with words from the scraps.

The sound of the _____ called the Israelites to gather at the foot of Mount

_____. The mountain sparked and shuddered, and Moses spoke to

_____, who responded in a voice that was heard in the _____,

the _____, the _____, and the _____. The voice

was like _____ voices that combined to become all the _____

spoken on earth. Thus, all who heard understood.

God   shofar   east   south   seven

north   Sinai   languages   west

With a pencil, trace the travels of the Israelites, starting with their exit from Egypt. Each stop is indicated by a dot on the map. Describe what happened to the Children of Israel at each stop.

Stop 1 _____

Stop 2 _____

Stop 3 _____

Stop 4 _____

Stop 5 _____

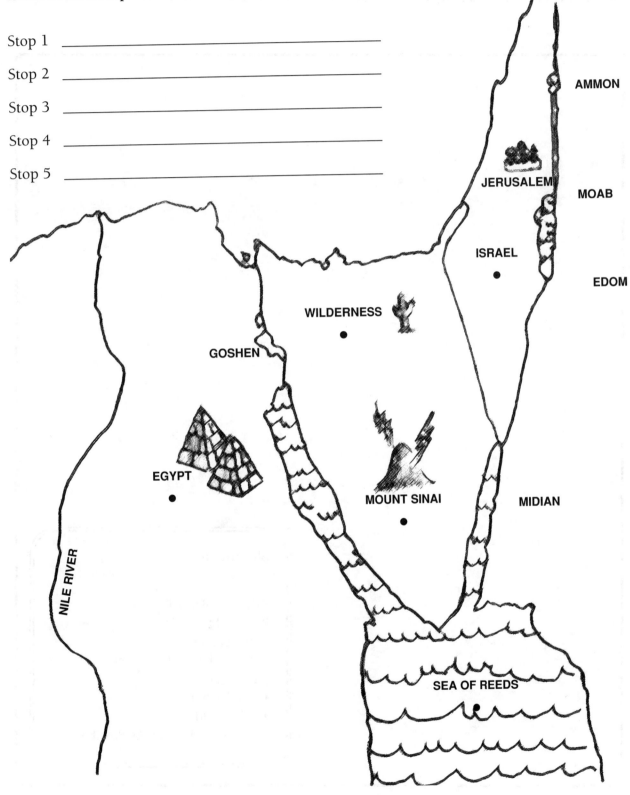

Blueprints are detailed drawings that craftspeople and artists use as a guide in building whatever they wish to create. From the description in the story, draw a blueprint of the menorah for Bezalel. Use your favorite colors to make it attractive.

Blueprint by _____
(your name)

Designer: Bezalel
Project: Menorah
Specifications:
• 6 Branches and a Center
  Column
• Candelabra
• Solid Gold
• Deadline: As Soon As Possible

The commandments have been shattered, and the pieces are all scattered. Rearrange the broken pieces of the first five commandments so they can be read.

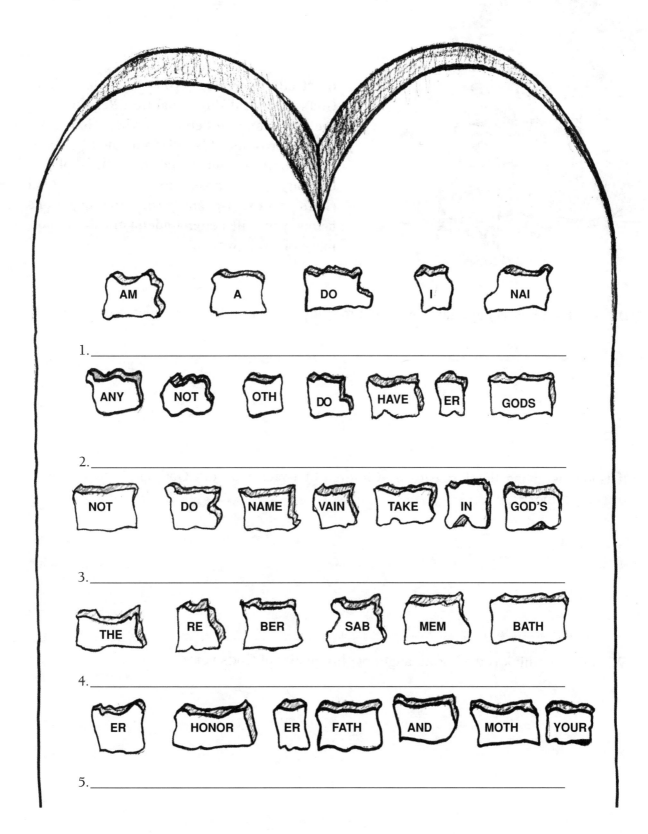

AM   A   DO   I   NAI

1. _____

ANY   NOT   OTH   DO   HAVE   ER   GODS

2. _____

NOT   DO   NAME   VAIN   TAKE   IN   GOD'S

3. _____

THE   RE   BER   SAB   MEM   BATH

4. _____

ER   HONOR   ER   FATH   AND   MOTH   YOUR

5. _____

F CUS QUESTIONS

In "God's Marvelous Voice," we learn that God's voice had three qualities: Regardless of age, everyone understood what God said; God's words and their wisdom could be heard everywhere at once; and regardless of the language they spoke, all could understand God's words. By answering the questions below, you will better understand the importance of God's words.

Do you think it is as important for a child to study Torah as it is for an older person? Why?

If God was giving the Torah to the Children of Israel, why did God speak all the other languages, too?

What do you think is the lesson taught by this quality of God's voice?

7 • Shall There Be One Law for Man and Another for Woman?

Fix the page of your "book" by filling in the blank spaces with the words in the scraps.

When Moses divided the land, he gave an equal piece to every _____. But

there were _____ fatherless sisters from the tribe of _____, who

had no brothers. So these sisters went to their local judge to request their portion of

land. But he didn't know how to judge their case—nor did the judges above him. The

sisters then went to the priest _____, who brought their case to Moses. But

even Moses did not know the answer. He went to the _____ to ask God,

and God responded: "_____ justice: This is the _____ of

Israel."

five   man   law   Eleazar

Tent of Meeting   Equal   Manasseh

FOCUS QUESTIONS

For this game, pair up with a friend. Choose who will be X and who will be O.

For these first two games, X gets to write in two X's on each turn, and O gets to write in only one O on each turn.

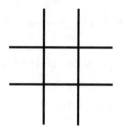 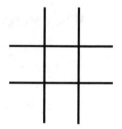

For these next two games, O gets to write in two O's on each turn, and X gets to write in only one X on each turn.

For these last two games, X and O can write in only one letter on each turn.

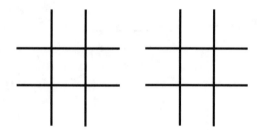 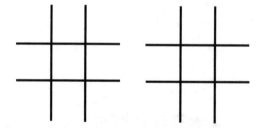

Who won which games? _____

Which were most fair?_____

Which set of games is like the law against which Zelophehad's daughters protested?_____

_____

Which set is like the law after God's decision? _____

The year is 2733. For your vacation, you have gone outside this galaxy to Planet Unequal Law, which has laws similar to those on Earth. You promised your mom you'd send her a postcard. Unfortunately, you didn't know that on this planet many of its laws are different for different people. For example, people with blue eyes can take the buses and trains, while people with brown eyes have to walk. On the postcard below, describe another unequal law to your mom.

If you need more space, continue here.

_____

_____

_____

_____

The two men pictured below used to be the best of friends. Then they had a major manna cart crash, and now they won't even speak to each other. Aaron wants them to make peace. Help Aaron by bringing each one to the center for a good hug.

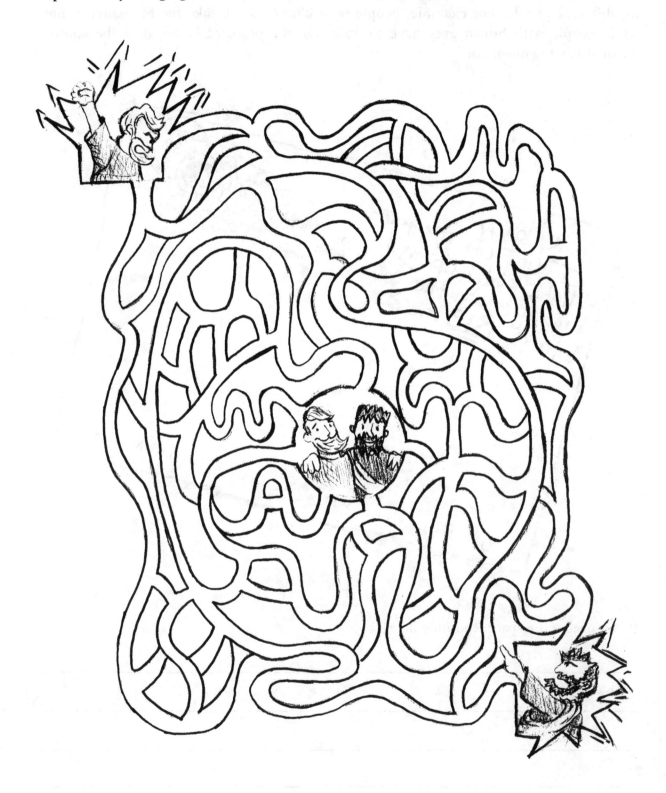

FOCUS ON PRAYERS OF THANKS

Sheesh! Those Jews were so ungrateful in the times of the judges! They should have thanked God for all that was done for them. In fact, giving thanks to God is another type of prayer. In the space below, compose a personal thank you prayer to God.

_____

_____

_____

_____

_____

_____

_____

_____

_____

8 • Deborah, Woman of Light

Here we go again! Fill in the blank spaces in your "book."

Deborah's husband's name was _____. Coming home from work very tired,

he would not be interested in _____. But she tried to encourage him to do

_____ deeds. From the wax she collected from _____, Deborah

made _____ for her husband to bring to the _____ who stud-

ied at _____. That is why God called her a "woman of _____"

and chose her to be a _____.

light   studying   good   judge   candles

scholars   Shiloh   Lappidoth   beehives

FOCUS QUESTIONS

Every group of people has a leader. Usually leaders have strong qualities that others admire. The history of the Jewish people is filled with leaders who had strong qualities. Without such leaders, the Jewish people would not have survived. Below are some questions about leaders for you to think about.

Name the leader you admire most.

What qualities does he or she have that you admire?

What qualities did Joseph have? Why did God pick Deborah to be a leader?

Why did God pick Moses to be a leader?

Deborah's one good deed led to many good deeds, just as throwing a pebble in a stream causes many ripples. A good deed is listed in each circle below. What consequences "ripple out" from that deed?

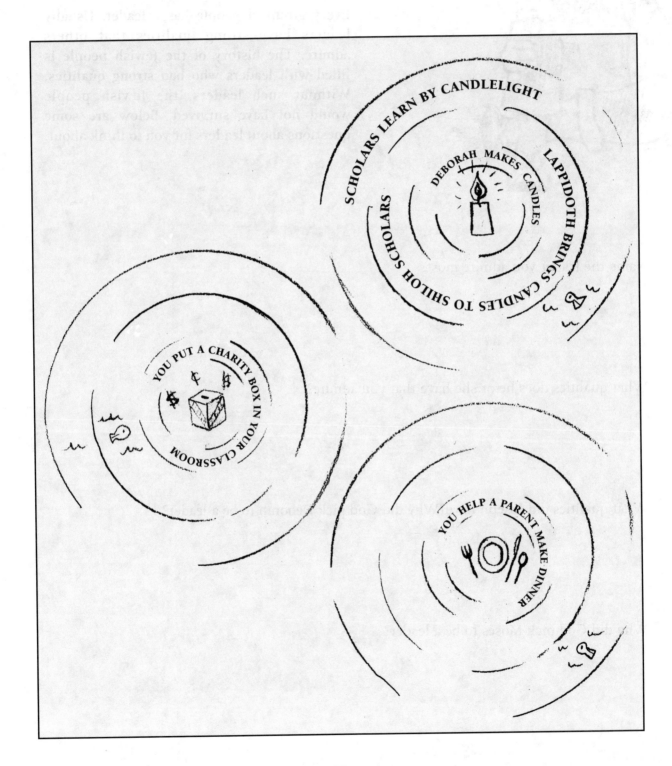

SCHOLARS LEARN BY CANDLELIGHT

DEBORAH MAKES CANDLES

LAPPIDOTH BRINGS CANDLES TO SHILOH SCHOLARS

YOU PUT A CHARITY BOX IN YOUR CLASSROOM

YOU HELP A PARENT MAKE DINNER

Naomi keeps discouraging Ruth from going with her, but Ruth is very determined. Help Ruth convince Naomi to let her go with her. On a separate sheet of paper, make a list of twenty questions based on what you have learned from all the chapters you have read so far. Then pair up with a friend. Each of you should choose a coin for a token and place it on the "Start Moab" circle. Take turns asking each other one question at a time. For each correct answer, move your coin two spaces forward. For an incorrect answer, keep the token where it is. The first one who gets to Israel with Naomi wins.

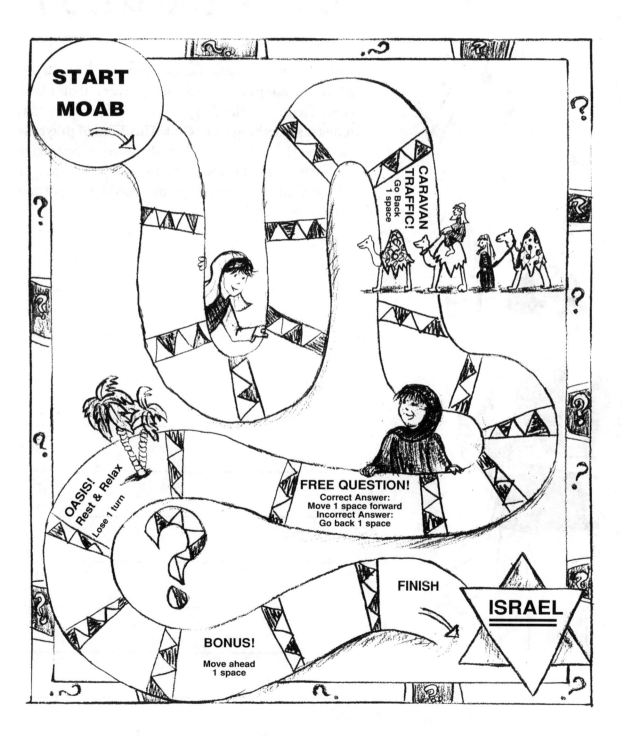

FOCUS ON PRAYERS OF REQUEST

So far we have spoken about two types of prayer: prayers that praise God and prayers that thank God. There is a third type of prayer: prayers that request something from God. This kind of prayer is the type Hannah made when she asked God to give her a child. In the space below, compose a prayer asking God for something you consider important enough to pray for.

_____

_____

_____

_____

_____

_____

_____

_____

_____

9 • King David Studies Torah

As you have done in earlier chapters, fill in the blank spaces in your "book" with the words in the scraps below.

King David enjoyed playing the _____. One night a _____ came

through David's window and played on his harp. David listened to the beautiful music and

decided to study the _____ scroll that was on his table. When the music stopped,

David turned from his studies and bragged about how great a _____ and

_____ he was. At that moment, a _____ came to his window and

told him not to boast so much since other _____ could sing even better than he.

King David realized that the frog was right, and they spent the rest of the evening singing

together, praising God.

Torah   harp   frog   breeze

scholar   singer   animals

Mr. Frog and King David are recording a CD entitled "King-n-Frog: Greatest Hits," to be released this Chanukah. Design their CD cover and write the song titles for the back of the CD.

GREATEST HITS

CROWN ARTISTS

KING
—N—
FROG

CROWN ARTISTS

1. _____ (1:23)
   (Song 1)

2. _____ (3:45)
   (Song 2)

3. _____ (6:13)
   (Song 3)

4. _____ (7:49)
   (Song 4)

5. _____ (10:10)
   (Song 5)

123456789

FCUS QUESTIONS

David listened to the frog and learned that all the world makes beautiful music! Think about the night when it's late and very quiet. Now imagine yourself going outside to listen to the sounds around you.

What sounds of nature do you hear? What man-made sounds do you hear, if any?

What are your favorite man-made sounds? What are your favorite natural sounds?

How do you think David would describe your favorite natural sounds?

How do you think David would describe your favorite man-made sounds?

Quick! David is hiding in a cave, and Saul is not far behind. Connect the dots so David will be saved.

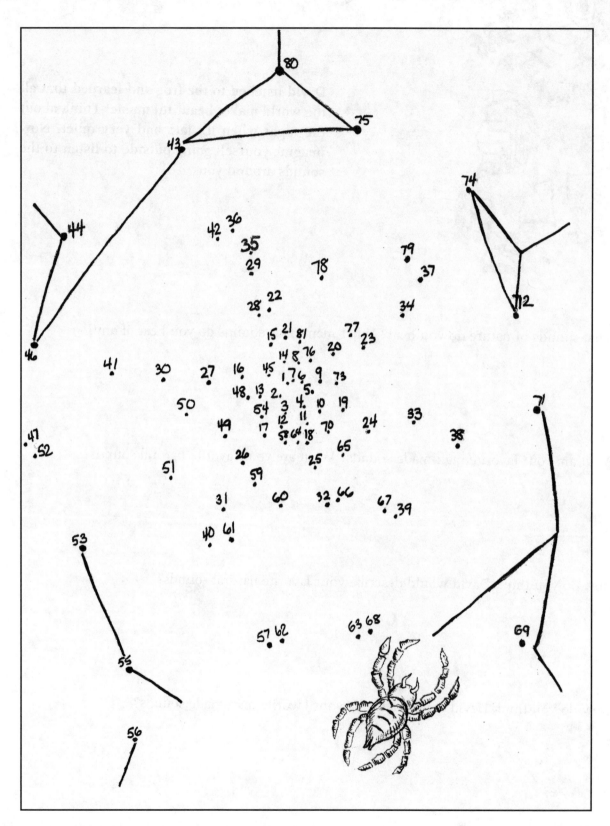

WBIB journalist Scoop Aggadah is interviewing three people about their eagerness to have a Temple. Unfortunately, Scoop forgot to turn on the sound, so we haven't a clue as to what the people are saying. Help us out by writing captions so the viewers at home can learn why these people are looking forward to having a Temple.

10 • Solomon and the Snake

Here we go again! Fill in the blank spaces with the words in the scraps.

One day a man met a _____ snake. In exchange for a drink of

_____, the snake offered to show the man where _____ had

been buried. But when the man tried to take the money, the snake tried to

_____ him. However, the man protested and insisted that they both go to

the _____ of King Solomon for a decision. Solomon ruled that while

the _____ says that snakes should kill men, men may also kill snakes.

Solomon then handed his _____ to the man, who used it to kill the snake.

milk   thirsty   kill

staff   court   money   Torah

46

Because of his great wisdom, King Solomon heard many cases in Israel. Some were probably more foolish than others. Below is one such case that may have been heard in Solomon's court. Pair up with a friend to complete the record of this case. Choose who will be the reader and who will be the writer. The reader will ask the writer to supply the kind of word called for (e.g., noun, verb, number). The reader will write that word in the blank space provided. Read the finished case together. Do not read the paragraph until all the blanks are filled in.

Hear ye! Hear ye! Court is   in session. In this case, the defendant is a

_____, who likes to _____.
      (noun—occupation)   (verb)

While doing this, the defendant _____ _____.
                          (verb, past tense)   (name of person in room)

The plaintiff now asks for compensation of _____ _____. The plaintiff
                                     (number)   (noun, plural)

further asks the court to have the defendant serve _____ hours of
                                             (number)

community service making _____.
          (noun, plural)

The Temple's light emanates and affects the whole world. Earlier we talked about how our actions have a ripple effect on subsequent events. Now we shall talk about how a community's actions can affect the rest of the world, just like the Temple's light. Label each ripple the way you did in chapter 8.

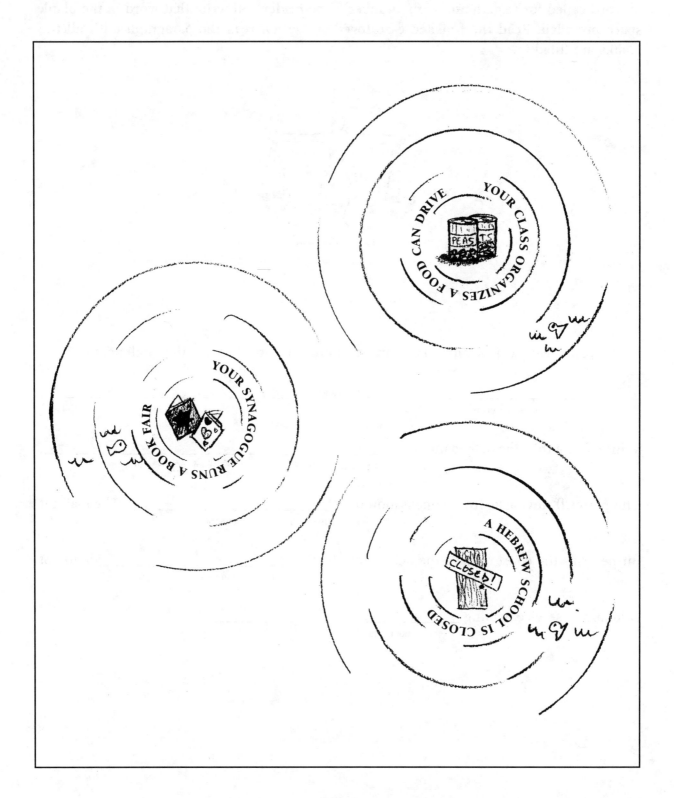

YOUR CLASS ORGANIZES A FOOD CAN DRIVE

YOUR SYNAGOGUE RUNS A BOOK FAIR

A HEBREW SCHOOL IS CLOSED

Remember the journal entries you wrote about small things? Well, meet the *shamir*, a very small fellow who made a very big difference. Right now, he's hiding below in a word jumble. Find and circle the words listed on both sides of the jumble. The words can go from left to right, from top to bottom, or diagonally. Unscramble the remaining letters to find the *shamir*.

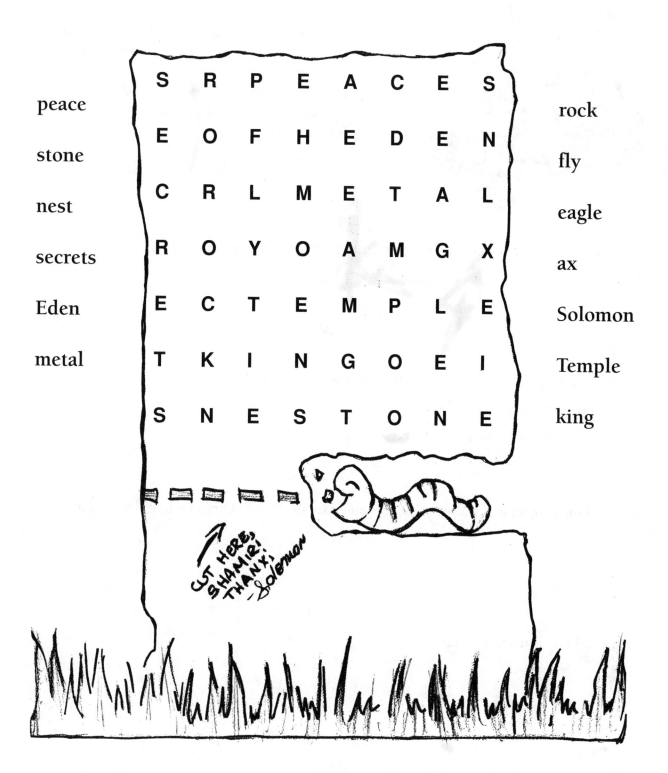

peace

stone

nest

secrets

Eden

metal

S R P E A C E S
E O F H E D E N
C R L M E T A L
R O Y O A M G X
E C T E M P L E
T K I N G O E I
S N E S T O N E

rock

fly

eagle

ax

Solomon

Temple

king

CUT HERE, SHAMIR! THANX! —Solomon

FCUS QUESTIONS

Many claim that David and Solomon were great kings because both were brave and wise. But even the wisest and the bravest have much to learn from the rest of God's creatures. Answer the following questions about learning from others:

What did David think was his greatest talent? From whom did he learn?

Solomon thought he was the wisest, but from whom did he learn?

Name three people, besides your teachers and parents, from whom you have learned things.

What did you learn from them?

11 • A Hundred Hidden Prophets

Fix your "book" again by filling in the blank spaces with words in the scraps.

After the reign of King _____, Israel was divided into the kingdoms of

_____ and Israel. The king of Israel was named _____, and he

married a woman named Jezebel. She was a wicked queen and brought

_____ into the Temple and the priests of _____ into the coun-

try. At that time, there were _____ prophets in Israel. When they all went

into _____, only the prophet _____ spoke out against Jezebel.

Elijah   idols   Ahab   Judah

hiding   a hundred   Ba'al   Solomon

51

Today, when Jewish couples get married, they often sign a *ketubah*. A *ketubah* is a marriage contract that lists the promises the couple makes to each other. In biblical days, there were no formal *ketubot*. If there had been, what do you think the *ketubah* signed by Deborah and Lappidoth or Ahab and Jezebel would have said? In the spaces below, write a *ketubah* for Deborah and Lappidoth and another for Ahab and Jezebel.

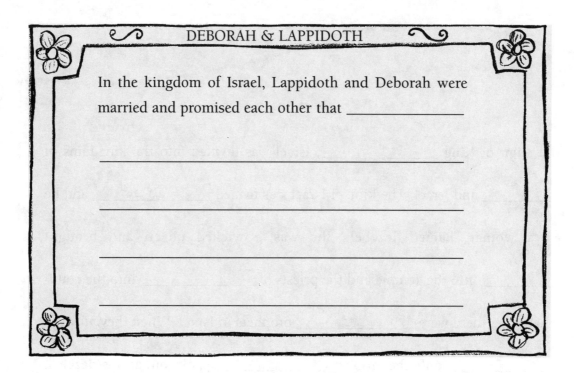

DEBORAH & LAPPIDOTH

In the kingdom of Israel, Lappidoth and Deborah were married and promised each other that _____

_____

_____

_____

_____

AHAB & JEZEBEL

In the kingdom of Israel, Ahab and Jezebel were married and promised each other that _____

_____

_____

_____

The ten lost tribes are really lost! Can you find them (Reuben, Simeon, Issachar, Zebulun, Dan, Naphtali, Gad, Asher, Manasseh, Ephraim) in the word jumble below? The words can go from left to right, from right to left, from top to bottom, from bottom to top, or diagonally.

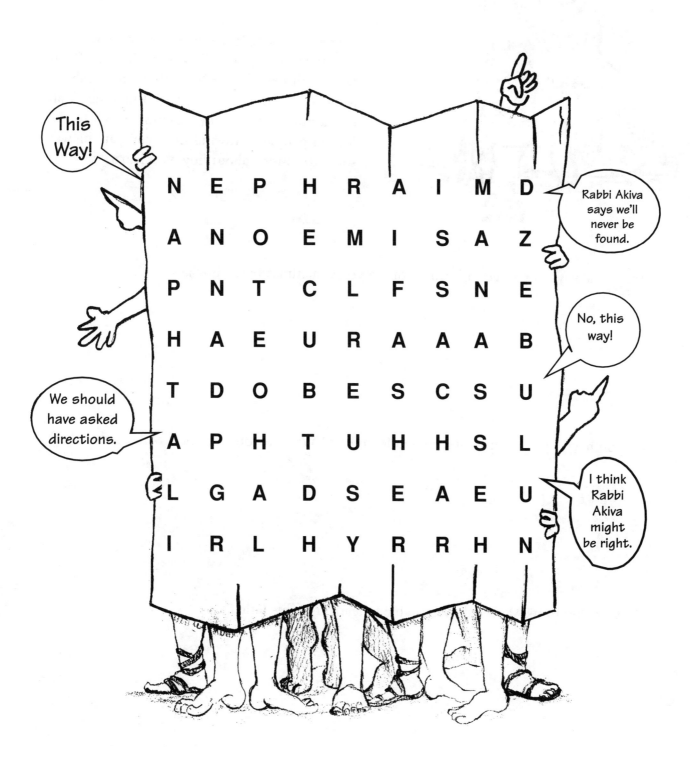

FCUS QUESTIONS

No one ever said learning would be easy. So we shouldn't be surprised to learn how difficult Manasseh made it for his father, Hezekiah, to teach him Torah. Fortunately, King Hezekiah had a much easier time teaching Torah to the Jewish people. Knowing that, you can answer some questions about how you learn.

Are you always interested in learning or are you sometimes bored in class?

Do you have a teacher from whom you learn best? Why do you learn best with that teacher?

Why do you think Manasseh wasn't able to learn from his father?

Scoop Aggadah is back again, reporting for WBIB. Below, he is interviewing three of the one hundred prophets who are in hiding. As usual, he is having sound trouble. We can hear his questions but not the answers. Write the prophets' answers below.

Why are you hiding?

What do you think of Jezebel?

Do you approve of how Elijah is handling the priests of Ba'al in Israel?

12 • Jeremiah and Moses

This last page of your "book" needs fixing. Complete this page, and you will have fixed all twelve pages. Great job!

When the Temple was about to be destroyed by the _____, God commanded his prophet _____ to summon Moses by calling out Moses' name from the banks of the river _____. When Moses appeared, he was informed that the Temple was to be destroyed. Moses then summoned the spirits of the _____ and _____. Together they went to the _____ of the Temple, their heads bent in _____. Only after God was certain that the Jews would hear words of _____ from their leaders was the Temple destroyed.

Jordan   gates   sorrow   Jeremiah   matriarchs

comfort   Babylonians   patriarchs

FOCUS QUESTIONS

Turn back to chapter 9 where you wrote the different responses from three people who were looking forward to having a Temple.

Do you think each one was happy when the Temple was finally built?

What do you think each one missed the most after the Temple was destroyed ?

Your textbook lists the different spirits called upon to comfort Israel. Pick one spirit for each of the three characters from chapter 9. Which spirit would be the best to comfort each character? Why do you think so?

FOCUS ON A PRAYER OF COMMUNITY

You have written personal prayers praising God, thanking God, and requesting something from God. In the space below, write a communal prayer. It should praise and thank God and request something not for yourself but for Jews everywhere.

_____

_____

_____

_____

_____

_____

_____

_____

_____

The third prophet taught us the square Hebrew letters we use for reading the Torah today. Every time a Torah is written, we are very careful that it is copied from another Torah in exactly the same way. In the grid below, copy, square by square, the very important phrase that appears in Hebrew on this page.

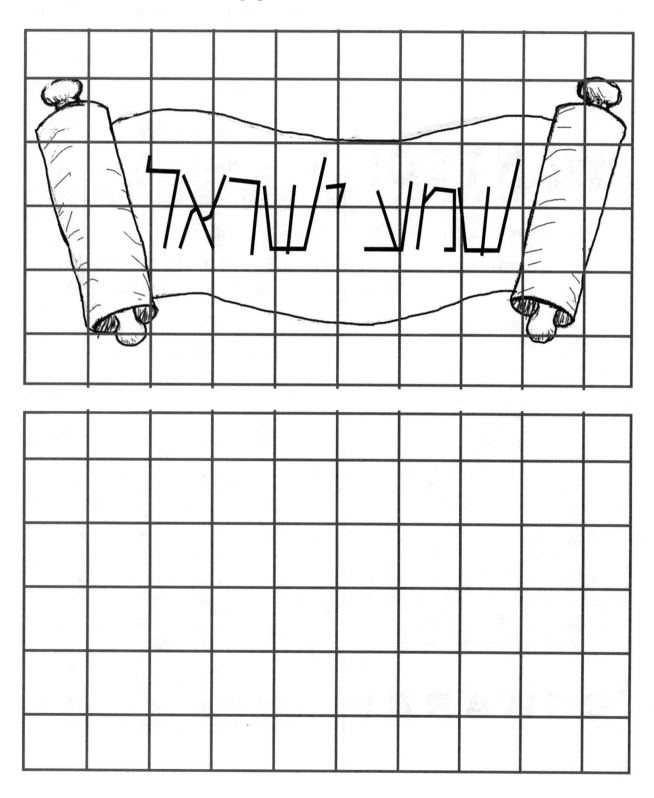

The Jewish people survived Haman and tons of other bad guys throughout history. Pair up with a friend. In the lines below, write the names of as many of those bad guys as you can think of.

Write a list of Jews that you know have contributed to making the world a better place in which to live. With the same friend, in the lines below, write the names of as many Jewish leaders, scientists, and heroes as you can think of.

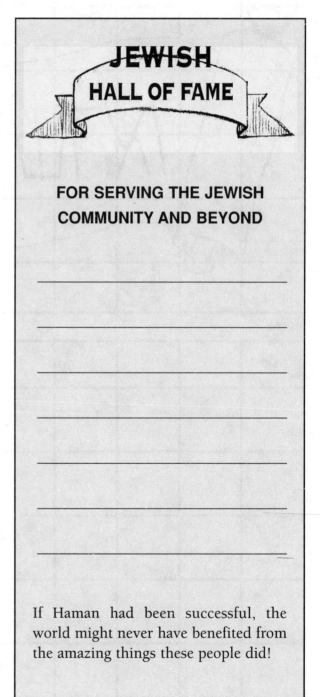

WANTED!

FOR CRIMES AGAINST THE JEWISH PEOPLE

—Sheriff

_____

_____

_____

_____

_____

_____

R E W A R D !

JEWISH HALL OF FAME

FOR SERVING THE JEWISH COMMUNITY AND BEYOND

_____

_____

_____

_____

_____

_____

If Haman had been successful, the world might never have benefited from the amazing things these people did!